THE PROBLEMS AMERICAN SOCIETY FACES IN THE 21st CENTURY
AND HOW TO FIX THEM

BY

DAVID JAMES ZOPPI

Contents

CHAPTER 10

CHAPTER 11

Preface

What ever happened to the carefree days of the 1950's when families like the one depicted in the popular television show "Leave it to Beaver" sat around the dinner table and actually *talked* to one another? We live in a new world, a sometimes impersonal world where technology has caused a disconnect where human interaction is concerned. It seems like we can say what we want and do what we want. Television, radio and platforms like concerts, plays and sporting events are being used to make political statements and our leaders are disrespected while Republicans and Democrats continue to play the *game* of politics at our expense where the side who does not have a president in power opposes the other sides policies; resulting in a unproductive political system. It is a world where civil unrest has re-ignited and our communities are divided and fragmented, a world where our inner-city youth needs more advantages and greater opportunities, a world where we live under the constant threat of terror and war, and a world where our privacy and personal information can be compromised by cyber threats from across the globe. We also live in a world where their needs to be greater acceptance of the rights of the LGBT community and awareness of transgender issues. In this book, I will discuss and analyze the many problems we face today in society and in the world, and how to potentially fix the problems

facing our society and the world before it is too late.

CHAPTER 1

The Good Old Days

What ever happened to the carefree days of the 1950's when families like the one depicted in the popular television show "Leave it to Beaver" sat around the table and actually *talked* to one another? In the 1950's there were sock hops, dancing, movies and ice cream soda shops and no computers, cell phones or texting. If you wanted to have fun, you made your own fun! Now a days, little Jonny is glued to the cartoon network and Daughter Sara is on her I-Pod while Mom and Dad are on their computers or other devices. Have families lost their cohesiveness today because of technology? I would have to answer yes to this. Families are not meant to be impersonal or distant to one another. The home is supposed to be a place of sanctuary, peace, harmony, tranquility and togetherness. But instead, there is a real disconnect between family members who allow technology to govern their lives as opposed to the 1950's for instance.

The reason I paint a much rosier picture of the 1950's is because there seemed to be a greater sense of family and much less civil unrest during this time than there was during the 1960's. Were there problems that people had to endure during the 1950's? Absolutely, in every revolution of time there are problems that we as individuals and as a society must face. In both decades America witnessed the unrest brought about by issues concerning unfair treatment and the rights of African Americans, and also the Vietnam War which caused unrest.

In the 1950's it seemed like husbands and wives tried to stick it out and avoid divorce, not only because of the sigma assigned to divorce during that time, but also for the sake of the children which meant foregoing happiness and enduring a not-so-perfect marriage for the sake of the children. While this may seem noble and admirable on the surface, I would still have to wonder how many of these marriages were *dysfunctional*. Sometimes, the noble thing to do in the long run may not be the right thing to do. Still, the 1950's projected an aura of a carefree time, a fun time and a time where great musicians and great music were born.

It was not until the 1970''s that we saw an era that almost mimicked the 1950's, the *Disco Age.* The disco age, as I like to call it, showcased music that was actually a throwback to the Latin beats and style of music, combined with distinct and elaborate dance steps and movies like "Saturday Night Fever" which sparked the disco craze and lots of wild and crazy outfits including the "Travolta Style" white suits with black shirts. Yes, this was a fun and memorable time as well which also gave birth to some great musicians and bands like: Barry Manilow, The Bee Gees, Kool & the Gang, The Commodores and others.

In-between the 1950's and the 1970's was the 1960's. The 1960's was a time of social revolution and civil unrest. There was the unfair treatment and the rights of African Americans, and also the Vietnam War as well as drugs like LSD, the draft, protests and the sexual revolution. This was also an era where great music and musicians were born such as: The Beetles, The Rolling Stones, Pink Floyd and others.

If you notice, in every era music was the great equalizer. It brought people together, it was an anchor and something to get people through the bad, chaotic and turbulent times. We can thank shows like: The Ed Sullivan Show, The Dick Clark Show and Soul Train for showcasing and giving rise to such great bands and artists and showcasing their work. While many turned to music as an anchor to ground them in troubling times, and a release from societal and personal problems, others turned to destructive outlets, like drugs and alcohol. The musicians Jimi Hendrix, Janis Joplin, Jim Morrison and Brian Cole all died from drug overdoses in the 1970's. In the 1960's hippies smoked marijuana, and heroin and LSD were the popular drugs of the time. So, while certain eras seemed to be carefree and good spirited, demons like drugs and alcohol were lurking in the background.

History should teach us valuable lessons and we should learn from our mistakes and not repeat them. However, it seems like we keep repeating some mistakes and repeating them over and over again. Instead of abstaining from using drugs like marijuana, some states have actually legalized its use. Are we becoming a country like countries such as Amsterdam where drug use is the norm? We have even come to see the birth of legalized gambling and being able to bet on horses online. What's next, legalized prostitution? Pornography online is out of control and with web cams and vile acts being carried out online virtually unregulated and uncensored, the online pornographic element is almost next of kin to legalized prostitution. Are we becoming a society that is now out of control?

We now live in a society that does not adhere to many of the morals, standards and values that kept us grounded in the past. In this *almost anything goes* society it is next to impossible to raise children to be moral and just when surrounded by immorality and uncivilized acts. We turn on the television and hear the words we teach our children not to say being said on television, or hear music with offensive lyrics that our children are subjected to. It seems like for a civilized society that we are in some ways regressing and moving backwards instead of forwards. Yes, there have been technological advances, but how little we have changed in some ways. We have made giants leaps forward and taken many steps backward.

When I see things like corruption, immorality, indecency, wickedness and evil, it only reminds me that good and bad exists here on earth. We as parents do our best to protect our children and ourselves from being corrupted by the bad things that are in this world, but sometimes it is difficult to do so. In this world that we now live in, sometimes the bad and the immoral are forced upon us through media and in society. Hence, we must now learn to take the good with the bad, and accept the fact that some aspects of immorality and inappropriateness are now the new norms for our culture.

Also, what can we do to make more quality family time for ourselves while not allowing technology to govern and rule our lives? As I mentioned earlier, we might consider the possibility that we are addicted to our technology, and if so this is a whole new area of psychotherapy to explore. We need to make time for other things in life besides texting, chatting and surfing the web. Day trips, museums, parks, the beach and other activities await those who can break the vicious cycle of being glued to technology day after day after day. Choose NOT to turn on the computer for one day or more, and substitute computer time with positive and constructive *family time.* "What did I accomplish today? This should be the question you ask yourself at the end of each day! If you have difficulty answering this question, then you need to take stock of your life, your goals and activities and see how you can make your time, the time you spend with your family and your life in general more productive.

CHAPTER 2

The Media, Social Media, Politics and Free Speech

It has been said that "When you have a kingdom divided against itself, the kingdom will fall. Politics can be thought of in these terms. When you have one side opposing the policies of the other side and opposing the president then very little can be accomplished without executive orders. When you witness a system of government and the 2017 "State of the Union Address" in which President Trump addressed the Congress and Democrats basically sat on their hands and refused to clap and/or stand, then this denotes a *system* divided against itself. When the system and the people in the system are self-serving and corrupted by power, money and greed, then how can the system thrive and serve the American people? When you have those that oversee others who are part of the system that fail to uphold justice and the law, then once again, we have to ask ourselves how such a system can thrive?

When those in power who have abused their positions and broken the rules go unpunished, it sets a poor example. It signals to those of us watching that perhaps being corrupt is acceptable, and this is wrong. We know we live in a morally upside down society when what is deemed wrong becomes right and acceptable. Other's break the rules and get away with it, so why can't I? What makes it even more confusing is that all the things we couldn't do in the past, we are *allowed* to do now! This has become a world and a society where we can find websites to bet online, we can find websites where we can find webcam women online, and we can use marijuana in certain states, hear profanity and see sexually explicit content on cable and satellite television. Why is this so? Because our society has to come extent become immoral these things are not only allowed, they are LEGAL!

Television broadcasts allow sexual content on television and pornography on paid television as well as profanity on television and the radio. Even some social media sites contain pornography and objectionable content. It seems like the FCC has also become much more lenient and tolerant because of the times we live in perhaps. We also have a media that thrives on sensationalism. The media is more like a mix of responsible news reporting and tabloid media. Leaks to the press have become more commonplace and the treatment of our leaders and those in high and powerful positions is tolerated in this country unlike other countries where such coverage of political leaders and presidents would not be tolerated.

One of the other freedoms we as Americans have enjoyed is freedom of speech. However, there is a difference between free speech and speaking in a manner that abuses that right and crosses the line. Just because we *can* say something doesn't necessarily mean that we *should* say what we want to say. Also, freedom of speech means *words* and not actions. When people use their positions as musicians, singers, actors and sports figures for instance to make political statements, then it takes advantage of a platform for which expressing ones' political views was not intended. When I go to church, I want to hear a sermon and not political views. When I go to a play or a sporting event, I do not want to see a public display of political opposition or hear someone's political views because that is NOT what I went there for. If someone wants to express their political views, they should do so through acceptable channels and platforms; such as letters to the editor or television and radio shows.

Freedom of speech also means not keeping someone else from talking with whom you do not agree with. We have seen in the news how speakers at colleges were met by protesters, and how politicians have been shouted down and their messages disrupted by protesters and those seeking to cause chaos and havoc. When our basic rights cannot be exercised and we are denied the right to speak and express our views, then it sends a clear signal that those things that we value and have valued as a nation are beginning to destabilize and become compromised. Order must not be substituted with chaos. Otherwise, we as a society will stand upon a foundation of instability.

We are a nation of opinions, and what better way to voice our opinions and make our stances on certain issues known is there than through social media. Social media is a wonderful place to post your opinions to news stories and other stories of interest, or to post an article of your own or your elaborated opinion on a particular story. However, social media and the internet are filled with people who would rather bully and insult others rather than having healthy and robust discussions on the issues. It has been said that "Insults are the arguments of those with weak and small minds". Hence, I and many other people I know who have made some comments on social media have been told to "shut up" and have been bullied and subjected to mean-spirited and hateful comments.

Unfortunately, trying to block all of these people is like trying to turn back the tide. It is a sign of the sad times we live in when groups of people can disrupt speakers from speaking and individuals can attempt to disrupt and silence other individuals on social media and other platforms just because they do not want the other person to express their point of view.

CHAPTER 3

Pornography in Our Society

Unfortunately, we are surrounded by pornography in our society. Exotic and Gentlemen's clubs, massage parlors, magazines, online and neighborhood stores and online content and services like webcams and chat rooms make pornography readily accessible and available. Because of the accessibility and availability of pornography, both live and otherwise, many in society are caught-up in a downward spiral. Some have become addicted to sex while others have allowed it to destroy their relationships and their lives.

Pornography has become so accessible that all we have to do is turn on our computer, pick up a phone and dial a sex talk line or order a movie on television through our cable or satellite provider and there it is! Yes, it is convenient, too convenient. Once again, we can take part in observing such content because society *condones* and *allows* it to a degree. Then, those who become addicted to such content find that they have created a home life that is dysfunctional. How can a parent raise a child to be a good and decent adult when that parent is acting counter to what is moral and decent? How can a man be a good father and husband when he is talking to women of objectionable character on webcams or in chat rooms? The same is true for women who are involved in this kind of work. How can a woman project herself as a decent mother and loving wife when doing work like webcam work?

Those who face such an addiction are the same people who you will find in church making confession and wiping clean their sins, only to return to the behaviors which lead them to confession in the first place and finding themselves locked in a vicious cycle of destructive behavior. To battle this addition and the sin associated with it, prayer and praying the "Act of Contrition" is not enough. Many people need counseling, but may fail to seek such help because of the stigma they may see associated with going to a counselor and may be afraid of being discovered.

We have seen people in positions of fame and in notable professions like Generals, Politicians and in show business whose careers have suffered and whose reputations have been tarnished and destroyed because they engaged in inappropriate behaviors which ultimately resulted in their downfall. Individuals both famous and not have engaged in these behaviors under the assumption that no one would ever catch them and no one would ever find out. Yet, the internet is not as secure as many would believe and still thousands of people post their personal information and engage in objectionable behaviors for the whole world to see, or to find out about.

As I stated, addiction cannot always be addressed with prayer and confession. I think that only the strong of will can overcome their own additions. However, when we need help, we must be willing and ready to turn to professionals who can help us to control and/or eradicate the behaviors that are causing us stress and destroying our lives and our very existence. When we fail to seek the help that we need and continue down a destructive path, then we assume the responsibility for the consequences of our actions such as loss of job, family, reputation and more. "We pay the price for the life we choose". Hence, we become responsible for our own downfalls. People need to find the strength to get the help they need when overwhelmed with a problem so great that it can't be conquered alone.

CHAPTER 4

Religion

We are a society built upon a foundation of ideals, beliefs and more. Religion instills faith and belief in us and in God. We believe that Jesus was born, lived and then died on the cross and took all the sins of humanity upon himself and saved us. There are many who hold dear their religious beliefs, and still others who do not believe. When we fall away from God, we fall from God's light and God's grace and essentially become like a lost sheep in the wilderness.

Religion if part of the fabric that holds society together. Those who do not walk with God walk alone and in darkness. When people fall away from God, or are at the other end of the spectrum and are evil doers, then good and bad are in a constant struggle for power and dominance in the world. The bad and the evil will seek to topple the good and the just, and the result can be devastating to societies and to our very civilization and way of life.

Societies and people need religion in their lives. Our religion and our faith give us something to believe in. Institutions, like religious institutions, give people faith and something to believe in. It is part of the *glue* that holds us together as a society.

In our churches, we can see the lack of religious participation. To ensure participation and make sure that religion remains a strong foundation and is tightly woven into the fabric of what holds our society and civilization together, we must understand *why* people are turning away from religion. Sometimes, when people seek out religion, they find that they do not like the rituals and rigidity of certain religions. Some like more singing, more dancing and more active participation, while still others want an experience that is more spiritual in nature and want to feel the presence of God and feel that they have been brought closer to God through religious participation. Therefore, people have begun to *shop around* for a religion that suits them and what they expect.

People have lost faith in institutions and with regard to religion, and we have seen a separation of church and state and religion and school. With no place for religion or politics in many of our schools some students are not free to pledge allegiance to the flag or hold true to their faith and to their religion. When freedoms are taken away, when options are diminished and excluded, then we do not become a free nation, but rather a nation that is controlled by government and institutions.

While religion and the Constitution of the United States are two separate entities and kind of like comparing apples to oranges, it is important to note that these are a few of the important elements of what we built our nation and our beliefs upon and what has held our nation together. Yet, some wish not to acknowledge religion or politics or allow the pledge of allegiance in our schools or stand for the national anthem to make a political statement, or because it does not fit into their belief system. It is fine to fly the flags of discontent and to hold *peaceful* assembly, but to oppose those who do not agree with it, to silence those in opposition to it, or to remove it from institutions like schools or sporting events can cause a great ripple of unrest across this land and create great chaos in our society. When we seek to destroy the things that contributed to the very foundation upon which our nation was built upon, then unrest, chaos and turmoil may eventually lead to the downfall of our society.

Another problem we have in general is a lack of faith. We have a lack of faith in our politicians, our law enforcement and religious institutions just to name a few. When we demonstrate a lack of faith or no faith in such institutions then how will these institutions survive? Also, if these institutions do not survive, then how will we survive? We need these institutions as much as they need us! In the case of religion, unfortunately there are too many people that do not feel that they need religion in their lives, and some people will choose to become atheists and choose not to believe at all.   There is actually a difference between belief and faith, but sometimes both terms are used interchangeably. When we believe in something, we are validating its existence. However, when we have faith in something, we are placing our confidence and our trust in something.

As a society, I think it is important to have faith in the positive. For instance, have faith in good, not evil; have faith in peace, not war, have faith in love, not hate. Why do we lose faith in the first place? Perhaps it is because one of these institutions has failed us, disappointed or upset us in some way. Or, perhaps one of these institutions has not met-up to our expectations. In any case, when we can affirm our faith in the positive and not the negative, then perhaps we can find the good in things that may not be quite perfect.

CHAPTER 5

Raising our Children to be Moral in an Immoral World

We only have to turn on the television or the radio to see adult situations or hear swear words or objectionable content or hear it presented in music. It has been said that "We're living in a world quite different from the one yesterday". The words we try to protect our children from hearing are being said on radio and television. We never know when we will flip to a channel and hear an objectionable word or see content not meant for young viewers. True, we can utilize parental controls, but the point is that if the world we live in were completely moral and decent then we would have no need for parental controls.

You can find people swearing on radio, on television, on the internet and in songs that our children listen to, and the message that society is sending to our young people is that some forms of immorality are permitted. A world without morality is like a world without laws to govern our behavior. This is what that world is like NOW! Just imagine what it will look like years from now, centuries from now if humanity survives and is not wiped out by a natural disaster, man-made calamity or extinction event like an asteroid.

Can we stop it? To this question my answer is NO! The forces of morality and immorality in our society and in the world are polar opposites and are like the forces of good and evil. While we can't STOP it, we can *control* it. Parents can filter what their children watch on television and monitor the type of music that their children are listening to on the radio. Research the artists and see if their lyrics use vulgarity or are offensive in any way, and then suggest other artists that the child can listen to.

To expand on this, musicians, vocalists, sports figures, actors and others are not just public figures to young people. They are role models, and the young listen to what they say and watch what they do. Notable public figures have great appeal and great influence on our youth, and because of this they *should* behave in a way and manner that promotes positive responses from our youth. However, when a famous public figure does something which is unlawful or immoral, it sends the wrong message to our youth. To a student of political science for instance, if that student sees a famous political figure rise to the seat of power through cheating, corrupt tactics, dishonesty and more, then it sends the message to that student that this is the same path that I must follow if I am to get ahead in that field.

Famous public figures who have a profound impact and influence on our youth have a *social responsibility* to act and behave in a manner consistent with demonstrating good morals and exemplary behavior. Those that do not need to be put on notice by the organizations and entities that employ them. Many organizations do this already. However, there are some famous public figures who have become too big for their britches and have evolved outside of the reach of censorship and justice and have essentially become *untouchable* and operate *above the law.* The rules do not apply to this class of people, and because of this, they can project an aura of immorality in the public eye and in their daily private and public lives.

To teach our children to be moral and to live moral lives, then we ourselves must live moral lives. How can we teach our children to be moral when we have become corrupted by the very things that we seek to protect our children from and teach our children to avoid? If we as parents cannot teach by example, then we are attempting to *mask* our own dysfunctional character behind an act. A corrupted parent can go to church, be a great and upstanding citizen of society who is well liked and respected by his or her fellow church goers and employees, but may be actually hiding a secret life and alternate lifestyle from family and friends.

The temptations of the internet and our own short-comings and vices can lead to our undoing as parents unless help is sought. When we can truly lead by example, then our children will truly benefit. We must be *genuine* to ourselves, our family and those around us. When our short-comings, human frailties and human weaknesses and vices take over our lives, it creates a home life which is dysfunctional and immoral. No matter how hard we try to project an image of morality, if we are immoral people, then we are just going through the motions at home, at work, at church and in life.

CHAPTER 6

Helping our Inner-City Youth

Every day many inner-city youth grow up in a world where they have and a mother who is struggling to make ends meet and are absent a father. As the children grow up into young adults, these inner-city youth experience violence, addiction, poverty and disadvantage. With nowhere to turn and no place to go, peer pressure lures some inner-city youth into gangs, drugs and more.

While children are the by-product of the mother and father, it is important to remember that when a child is born into the world that they are *separate* living organisms. No matter how much we as parents wish our children to follow our advice and make the right decisions in life, we must respect our children's choices and decisions when these decisions and choices are right for *them,* and not chastise or discard our children when they make the wrong decisions in life, or make decisions that we as parents do not agree with or approve of.

A young adult will make a number of decisions in his or her life that the parent or parents may or may not agree with. Such decisions might include: choice of college, not going to college and choosing to work instead, buying a new car, gender identification and sexual preferences, moving to another town or state, marriage, marriage inside or outside of ones' race; which are all right choices for the person making them but may be choices and decisions that the parent may or may not agree with. But what happens when a young adult chooses to use drugs, alcohol, hang out with gangs, drop out of school or make the wrong choices in life? First and foremost, we as parents must NEVER kick our kids out, disown them or push them away or aside. When our children make the wrong choices' we must give our children the love and support that they need and also find the help and interventions that they need. Too many children run away from home, are discarded by their parent or parents or come from homes where the family is a dysfunctional one. Our inner-city youth needs guidance, love, support and assistance to succeed in life.

With the strategies, skills and resources to succeed, people can find and educate themselves to create and take advantage of opportunities. However, when the disadvantaged have little to no skills and resources and lack the strategies necessary to succeed, then what can be done? In every inner-city, non-profit teen centers should be established to help young adults with skills like resume writing, job search and interviewing skills, computer and reading literacy and opportunities to complete High School for those who have dropped out to obtain a GED. For those who have received their GED, assistance with applying to colleges, universities or trade schools can also be provided as well as employment development. Computer labs could also be established for young adults to avail themselves of.

Such a center might also include a recreational component such as basketball and/or exercise facility and a social worker on staff for instance. There is a saying that states that: "Work must balance out with play, and sleep and rest must balance out with work". Therefore, when working with inner-city youth and training/re-training individuals to transition to work, trade school or college, I believe that there needs to be a balance. Education and job development and recreation must balance out. There would also need to be rules that govern the use of the recreational facilities. Participants would need to commit a certain number of hours to education and job development in order to use the recreational facilities, and using the facilities for recreation alone should not be allowed.

The purpose of such a facility should be to get the inner-city youth off of the streets, away from unsavory elements and bad influences and involved in educational, job development and recreational services that will benefit the person and give him/her a chance to get the skills, education and training needed to succeed and to create a better future. There are too many young adults that are being held back by life circumstances. However, the creation of such centers in each and every inner-city across the nation will give inner-city youth new hope for a brighter future.

It has been said that: "Men and Women are four: He/she who knows not and knows not he/she knows not, he/she is a fool—shun him/her; He/she who knows not and knows he/she knows not, he/she is simple—teach him/her; He/she who knows and knows not he/she knows, he/she is a sleep—wake him/her; He/she who knows and knows he/she knows, he/she is wise—follow him/her". There are those inner-city youth who may already think that they have life all figured out, and that the way they are going to get by is to keep everything as it is and not try to seek change in their lives. Still others may want desperately to break away from the poverty, the drugs and the crime and want to be taught so that they can take control of their lives. Still others have hidden gifts and potential yet to be explored and developed and need people and services to help them to discover this hidden potential. Others are born leaders who can and will succeed given the skills, the tools and the opportunity to do so.

In order to succeed, there needs to be community outreach. Not every inner-city teen or their parent/s may know where to turn, so outreach workers need to have lists of High School dropouts and lists of students with high absentee rates at High School and then go into the homes, to gangs, and go into the schools and give talks and get the word out verbally, on signs, bill boards and in other effective ways.

Not only should inner-city teens be assisted, but the parent or parents need to receive assistance as well. Social workers need to assess the home situation and then determine what supports are needed in the home to support the teen and the parent or parents. Parenting programs, financial assistance, food stamps, job assistance and training as well as other services may be needed to help a parent or parents to provide a stable home life and a solid foundation on which to sustain a family and raise a child.

This problem needs to approached and confronted on many fronts if inner-city youth are to rise above the status quo and succeed in life. The family is the foundation on which the success or failure of inner-city youth programs depend. If there is drug use or alcohol use in the home or an abusive home environment or even peer pressure to use drugs from fellow gang members for instance, then it may not matter what kind of training or programs the inner-city youth is involved in. Without a safe and stable home life and life outside of the home, the distractions and temptations may be too great. Problems on the home front need to be addressed and resolved first if any interventions are to be successful. Otherwise, the odds of success may be greatly diminished.

How then does addressing the problems of our inner-city youth contribute to averting the downfall of American society? Humanity can crumble for many reasons. Financial, political, social and outside forces can compromise our nation's ability to thrive and to grow. When we see a homeless person or someone seeking help, we must look deeper to determine the circumstances that lead to the homelessness or that lead to a life of crime or disadvantage and then attempt to find solutions to remedy the problems and to fix them. Some people seek help, while others seek assistance to get back on their feet, while sadly still others seek hand outs and have no intention of trying to improve their life and quality of life. Therefore, we must also learn and identify not only the problems that lead to inner-city youths getting involved in violence, crime, drugs, absenteeism or dropping out of school for instance, but also determine the reasons for why their current situation exists and what they have done, failed to do or chosen not to do to improve their lives and why. If it is merely a matter of not knowing where to go or who to seek out for assistance, then inner-city youth and their parent/s or care givers need to receive education, training and supports to find the help and assistance that they need.

CHAPTER 7

A New System of Incarceration

In the previous chapter, I discussed the importance of assisting inner-city youth and their families so that inner-city youth can receive the assistance, education and training that they need to improve their lives, find jobs and go to college while parents and care givers receive the parental training, help and supports they need to provide a stable home life. However, what happens when parents and/or inner-city youth are unable or unwilling to change and positively improve the condition of their lives? When the situation remains unchanged and just gets worse, an unstable home life can lead to inner-city youth running away from home or entering a life of crime, which can lead to jail.

When all else fails, our nations prisons do not have to be a place of stagnation and non-growth for the inmate. Jail time does not have to mean stagnation for inmates who have the potential to grow and to change their lives if and when they return to society. Vocational, educational and interest assessments can help to identify what kind of jobs an inmate may be suited for. For those prisoners who show promise and demonstrate good behavior, perhaps they could be accompanied by prison staff to a worksite daily to perform a job, receive training and perhaps transition into that job or job related to the one that is being performed after leaving prison.

For instance, let us use the example of an inmate who wishes to learn the trade of an auto mechanic. For this to occur, each prison would have to have as part of the prison a trade school for inmates to attend daily. After successful graduation, job development staff would find the inmate a job working with staff who would accompany the inmate to and from the work site. After the inmate is released, he/she would transition into the job that they had been doing as a full or part-time employee. Job assistance, job development and if necessary, job placement would also be available to the inmate as well as workshops in resume writing and interviewing skills.

As you read this you may be asking why a jail should offer these opportunities to inmates. If an inmate does nothing to improve himself/herself while in prison, then the possibility of recidivism and the ex-convict to relapsing and returning to prison always remains a possibility. When inmates who hold the potential and the promise to change are given a chance to improve themselves through *rehabilitation,* the hope is that the recidivism rate will go down and the released inmate will not return to a life of crime and to prison.

While there are many in the prison population that can be helped and rehabilitated, there are still many others who cannot be helped. Those who are amoral are far beyond rehabilitation. Amoral individuals are the worst of the worst. Examples of amoral inmates are: murders, rapists, serial and mass murders. Also, when amoral behavior is accompanied by psychotic behavior for instance, it can make such individuals even farther beyond reach because these are lost souls that have descended into the great abyss and are lost in a void so dark and so deep and immense that nothing and no one can reach them or help them.

For those that can be helped, it is important that all the work that an inmate does while in prison to better himself or herself is not in vain once leaving prison. By this, I mean that employers need to change their attitudes and the way in which they perceive those who have served time in prison. Employer bias needs to be put aside and those who have served their time in the prison systems need to be given a chance to reclaim their lives and get a fresh chance at making a new, positive start. One such way in which to change an employer's attitude toward hiring ex-convicts might be to offer incentives such as tax breaks! Also, some companies ask potential employees to take surveys that ask questions such as: "Have you ever stole anything"? If an ex-convict answers in the affirmative to any of these survey questions, the employer should and must allow the ex-convict to still interview for the job and clarify any 'yes' answers to any of the survey questions submitted.

Just as important rehabilitation is, it is equally important to allow flexibility in sentencing of inmates for good behavior and progress made in rehabilitation and transitioning back into society. Just because someone is sentenced to five years in prison for committing a crime shouldn't mean that they should have to serve the entire five years if they have been rehabilitated and have demonstrated good behavior, progress and show promise in being able to transition back into society.

It costs thousands of dollars every year to feed and shelter and care for prison inmates. We as a society need to partially turn away from incarceration and imprisonment and look toward implementing *rehabilitation and re-integration* interventions. We need to help those incarcerated get the education, training, job supports, social services and help and assistance that they need to re-enter and re-integrate back into society as quickly as possible and become productive citizens with less chance of returning to prison. If young people who enter prison couldn't get the help they needed on the *outside*, then they need to be able to get that help that they need on the *inside.*

Some may argue that when someone is sent to prison that they should be punished and not be given the opportunities for growth and development, for education, vocational training and work. True, there are some as I stated that are beyond help, beyond rehabilitation and cannot be turned around and rehabilitated. However, prison does not need to be a place of stagnation. Criminals do not have to leave prison no better than they entered. Prison should not develop into a way of life for those who become *dependent on the system.* The reason for rehabilitation and for helping prisoners is to try to ensure that they will not come back.

To help ex-convicts succeed, there also needs to be interventions in place after they leave prison. They cannot just be cut loose without a net initially. This means that counseling, social services, job and family supports and assistance needs to be made available to help ex-convicts make as smooth a transition back into society as possible. For those without families to return to when leaving prison, this could mean going to a group home-type setting similar to a half-way house. The difference would be that it would NOT be a half-way house, but a permanent situation for those without homes to go to. Recently released inmates would work and a portion of their income would be set aside for food, utilities, rent, etc. If an ex-convict in one of these group home settings were to re-commit a crime for instance, then that ex-convict would be returned to prison when apprehended if he/she committed a crime or did something which would constitute being returned to the penal system.

These group homes would be supervised and transportation would be provided to those in the group home to and from work sites unless that person were to purchase his/her own vehicle or utilize public transportation. While the half-way houses were the half-way mark between integrating back into society, the group home setting could be used for those cases that may prove at a high risk for returning to prison because of not having family on the outside or having a record of frequently retuning to prison. These ex-convicts would not have to go to such a group home, but it would be suggested as an option to those who would benefit. In addition, those who enter this living arrangement would not be required to stay. It is only suggested as an alternative for those who might benefit and who lack the resources and opportunities on the outside and are at risk of returning to a life of crime.

CHAPTER 8

Maintaining Order to Amidst Chaos

We are a nation of laws and we have rules that help us to abide by those laws. Law enforcement is the only thing that stands between peace and a lack of civic order and perhaps even anarchy and chaos. When there are deep divisions and divides between the police and the communities they serve, civic and community leaders and law enforcement need to come together to find ways to address the problems that face those communities while improving relations between the police and the communities that they serve.

Those who enforce our laws must be given the tools and the support that they need to do the job of keeping order and protecting the peace. In the case of protests that have turned into civil unrest and the destruction of property, we have seen incidences recently where the National Guard had to be called in to assist the police in restoring order and keeping the peace. This is what can happen and what does happen when peaceful assembly turns into chaos.

Citizens have the right to protest and the right to peaceful assembly. Protesting does NOT give anyone the right to destroy, to agitate or to resort to violence. Doctor Martin Luther King encouraged protests to be conducted in a manner that were passive, non-aggressive and non-resistance. Violence and destruction and seeking to silence those whose views that may be different from our own is not the way to get our own points and stances across. Violence only begets violence and this course only obscures the message of any protest or rally. Marching by the masses, holding signs and rallies to make messages heard are all effective and acceptable ways in which people can hold *peaceful assembly* and *peaceful protests.*

Not only is the freedom to protest and the right to hold peaceful assembly a right that we as Americans enjoy, but also the right to Freedom of Speech. However, just because we *can* say something doesn't necessarily mean that we should say what we want to say if it is hurtful, offensive or objectionable. Nonetheless, we must hear people out because we are *a nation of opinions.* We must have the freedom to speak and to allow others to speak and to state their opinions and then judge their words accordingly.

One of the best places to state opinions and react to news stories, stories of interest and opinions to each other's stories and posts is through social media. However, there are some people in the world who believe that freedom of speech means shouting down the other person and keeping them from delivering their message, or telling others with whom they disagree on social media to essentially "shut up" and/ or becoming verbally abusive to the point of bullying the person making the comment or post, just because they don't like or disagree with what the other person is saying. Freedom of speech *doesn't* mean that I can talk and you can't. Freedom of speech *doesn't* mean that you can use violence, agitate others to commit violence through your words and/or actions, and freedom of speech *doesn't* mean that you can destroy public property to get your message across. Freedom of speech is defined as: *"The right to any opinions without censorship or restraint"*. However, when that basic right is embellished upon by incorporating other elements into the definition like: *Free speech backed-up by senseless violence,* or *free speech backed-up by destruction of property* then the original definition becomes convoluted and invalid and takes on a meaning quite different from the one intended.

Our humanity has evolved technologically, but in some ways our world has remained the same. There is still war, terror, famine, vileness and corruption in the world and if Jesus were to come back to judge us, he might discover that in many ways, we have not progressed much in the last 2000 years. We now live in a technological age. Gone are the days of the telegraphs, rotary phones, cassette tape players and bulky stereos our parents owned that played 33, 45 and 78 size records. We now live in the computer age and the age of the internet. While the internet is a wonderful tool for learning, exploring and discovering, the internet can also be an unsafe environment. There are those who have learned how to exploit the internet, compromise your personal information and e-mail accounts and actually hold your computer for ransom in exchange for a payment to free your computer!

Hence, with this new age of cell phones, I-pads, computers and more, we always have to keep on the alert for cyber threats, viruses, hackers and more.

Because of such technology, our privacy is now compromised. Our emails, our personal information and financial information held by institutions like our banks, the places we shop online and more are all vulnerable, as is our very nation and its infrastructure. Even our webcams and our Wi-Fi devices are not safe. So, what can we do to protect ourselves?

Government and big companies hire cyber-security firms to monitor and manage cyber-security for them. However, as common citizens not all of us can afford to pay for that level of monitoring and security. But, there are steps that we can take to protect ourselves when online and offline. If you have a firewall that was initially installed with your computer, then it is a good idea to check it regularly. Sometimes, when we install other anti-virus software, it can affect the firewall. So, check your firewall often. Also, make sure that you have a strong password for your router and make sure it is working properly. Recently, I had trouble connecting to the internet and discovered that my older router from the company I purchased it from needed a fix which I found online. So, check your router and Wi-Fi devices and security often. If you don't know how to do this, then call a professional to do an evaluation and assessment for you. In addition to these things, having a strong anti-virus program installed in addition to the firewall is absolutely essential. There are so many anti-virus programs out there that finding the right one can become perplexing and confusing. Therefore, if you don't already have adequate anti-virus protection, or are confused about which one to choose, ask around and perhaps ask computer stores and/or technicians about the best choices that are on the market today.

Today, it is the age of the computer and tomorrow it will be the age of the robot. Artificial intelligence has already taken over many tasks, eliminating jobs at supermarket check-out lines and in factories where automation and machines are doing the work that humans once did while assisting humans in completing job-related tasks and more. It is believed that by the year 2020, many Americans will have robots in their homes. It wasn't too long ago that people could do long division and other complex calculations with a pencil and a piece of paper and actually use card indexes to search for a book in a library. Then came computers and calculators and our work was made easier, but what has it done to our minds and our motivation. I remember on one occasion walking into a fast food restaurant. The people behind the counter taking orders were lost because the power had went out and they didn't know how to make change without the cash register doing it *for* them. Is this what have to look forward to? Computers, calculators, robots and more doing work for us and replacing human beings? Computers serve us well and I am sure that robots will be excellent servants.

However, I have no desire to serve one or allow a robot to take away my job or work that I enjoy doing. Part of the reason that we desire to work is that it gives us a sense of *purpose* in life and personal satisfaction in a job well done. We are committed to our work, our companies and our employers as well as our co-workers. Satisfaction, loyalty, commitment and purpose are all things that *humans* know and feel and could never be part of the make-up of a robot. When you take away the *human* element you are essentially ripping the heart out of the organization.

It has been suggested that at some point in time, the human soul will be able to be transported into computers resulting in a way to achieve immorality. The day that men and women transform into machines and when robots become sentient beings is the day that all of humanity will change. Humanity will take a direction that perhaps God did not intend it to when the souls of the deceased are transferred into computers and robots develop the ability to think and to reason as effectively, or better than we can.

To bring order to science and technology as it applies to our world and the way it could help, or hurt humanity, we need to think before we act. We need to project ahead into the future and consider all possible outcomes including the risks and the benefits to humanity. Then, we need to examine the moral and ethical implications of what we will do before we do it. We must never allow technology to grow beyond our capacity to control it, and we must never allow technology to potentially replace humanity. If humanoid robots with artificial technology develop the capacity and the ability to think and to reason independently and when robots replace humans in work-related roles then we will have reached the *END* of human potential. By this, I mean that when machines and sentient humanoid robots that can think, reason and conduct themselves independently of humans and do everything for us, then we will have destroyed the reason for our very existence. We as humans need to explore, to have meaning and purpose in our lives and to develop and grow and have challenges both intellectual and otherwise. Technology should be present in our lives to serve us and to make our lives easier, but NEVER to replace us.

As I mentioned, we must also not let technology grow beyond our capacity to control it or other countries to use the same kind of technology to monitor and to control us. Nuclear and cyber technology are two such examples. Because we do not have the ability to control other nations actions, unfortunately those nations who possess advanced nuclear and cyber-threat capabilities and use or threaten to use these against their neighbors or other countries including the U.S. could obliterate other countries, bring down power grids, communications and more.

To counter such threats, in addition to sanctions there must be a unified front of civilized countries that make it clear to uncivilized countries that bully and intimidate others using such technology and weapons that there will be consequences. When we handle dangerous chemicals, we may use rubber gloves, and when we walk with a knife, a pair of scissors or even a riffle, we keep all of these pointed down to the ground in a safe position. We do this not only for safety sake and for precautionary measures, but also because we must exercise *responsibility* when using such things so that we do not hurt ourselves or anyone else. The same is true of technology. We must use it safely, responsibly and in a manner that does not hurt us or hurt *or threaten* anyone else.

CHAPTER 9

Confronting Corruption and Big Business

How much have we suffered at the hands of big business and industries that wish to keep us down and in the dark? It is difficult to say. Let us assume that someone built a car that could run on water and travel 2,000 miles on a tank of water. Now, let us further assume that an auto industry giant bought the rights to the patent and buried it so that it would never see the light of day. Next, let us assume that stem cells could help heart attack patients by healing damaged hearts and giving them a new lease on life, or regenerate the severed spinal cords of accident victims and allow them to walk again!

Can you imagine what would happen if a car that could run on water were brought to market? The car giants who make cars that run on gas, diesel and electric as well as hybrid cars would go out of business; as would the gas stations that sell the gas to fuel such cars. Can you imagine what would happen if there were a treatment using stem cells that regenerated damaged tissue and allowed people to walk again, regenerate their hearts and other organs and eliminate the need for wheel chairs and certain medications? The drug industry and other industries would face financial disaster. Now, imagine if everything I just told you were TRUE!

There are doctors that can regenerate new organs and heal the sick with the use of regenerative medicine, and yet, this type of new pioneering medicine may not be available for another 10 years here in the United States. Can you imagine if damaged and failing organs, hearts, livers and spinal cords could be repaired and/or replaced? It would not only affect the big pharmaceutical companies and those companies that make wheel chairs and other products. It would affect care givers, doctors and nurses. Let us not stop there! Because it would more than likely increase our lifespan, it would affect our food and water supply because the world's population would be out of control, it would also affect insurance companies, social security and so much more. Companies, government entities, big businesses and industries like drug companies who would lose *billions and billions* of dollars

When such inventions and medical miracles are buried or prevented from seeing the light of day then the drug industries and others will continue to profit off of the sick and the dying. How can we as common citizen's speed-up the process or avail ourselves of the research that is out there? To speed-up the process of seeing such inventions, cures and promising interventions brought to the forefront, we can certainly write a letter to the editor. When we write a letter to the editor of our local newspaper, we are essentially voicing our opinion before hundreds and thousands of people. Sometime, people of influence may read your article and be moved by what they have read, be moved to action or reach out to you.

When I wrote such a letter to the editor about stem cell research I was surprised to receive a call from the newspaper that I wrote to. When I returned the call, the person that I spoke to asked me if they could give my phone number to a man who enjoyed reading my article and who wanted to reach out to me. So, writing a letter to the editor can be a very effective way to tell the world how you feel. You can even write your senator on issues of importance and tell them what your concerns are.

Aside from speeding-up the process, another way to avail yourself of such research is to actually *become a part of the process.* By going on the internet and doing some research on stem cell therapy clinical trials, you can find an abundance of information. However, because the internet is filled with sources both credible and not, it is important to discuss any clinical trial research you find with your doctor before signing-up for it. Research and investigate what you find and then discuss it with your doctor. Then, if your doctor approves it, the next step is to ask lots of questions of those who are doing the clinical trial.

I recently inquired about getting involved in a clinical trial involving stem cells that heal heart tissue because of a heart attack that I suffered in 2013 which caused heart damage. The trial was approved by my doctor and cardiologist and then I asked those who are doing the clinical trial many questions to learn the risks and the benefits of the procedure. For example, some of the questions that I asked were: What is the objective of the clinical trial? What are the possible long-term effects on those patients treated? Could my heart stop during the procedure? Will I have heart palpitations during or after the procedure? Where will the stem cells be taken from? What are the odds that I will receive a placebo instead of the actual stem cells? Do those who receive the placebo get saline solution injected into the heart? Do I have to take medications other than my own? Is there a possibility that I will suffer nerve damage when stem cells are taken from my hip? Is there any cost to me for participating in the clinical trial? *You get the picture?* Ask lots and lots of questions! When we actively become part of the process or take an active role in trying to speed-up the process, either individually or collectively, we are saying in one voice or in one collective loud voice ENOUGH IS ENOUGH. Too many people are suffering, too many people are dying. If a cure or promising treatment is available, then let's have it!

CHAPTER 10

Terrorism

December 7, 1941 was: "A Day which will live in Infamy" which were the words that President Franklin D. Roosevelt said to a Joint Session of Congress a day after the Japanese Empire attacked Pearl Harbor. America had been attacked by a foreign power, and it wouldn't be until September 11, 2001 that America would be attacked once again. On that tragic day the twin towers in New York were brought down by commercial aircraft hijacked by terrorists, and the Pentagon building was crashed into by a commercial aircraft also hijacked by terrorists.

Since that day, we have seen an increasing number of terrorist attacks across the country and around the world. As a nation, Lady Liberty has held her torch up high and has welcomed immigrants to this country who have made a new life for themselves, started families and businesses and more. As a result, we have a society rich in cultural diversity. However, as a result of terrorism, some in government have sought to ban certain ethnicities from entering our country. It is a shame, because an entire race of people should not be punished because of the actions of a few. Instead of banning an entire race, we need to look at the immigration system as a whole to determine flaws in the system.

The interviewing and application process needs to be backed-up by investigation. When a person is asked on an application if they have ever committed any acts that would be considered terrorism, if that person answers 'no' then do we take that person at their word? Or, do we investigate further? If a person enters or tries to enter this country illegally, if someone's identity and background cannot be found or if a person has a criminal or questionable background, then this should be the type of criteria for not allowing someone to enter the country.

Those who have already been in this country should be allowed to stay and to apply to adjust their undocumented or non-legal status to legal, permanent status. Unless the person has a criminal background, that person should be allowed to make amends through applying for a change of status through the immigration process. To go out and round-up all the undocumented immigrants and send them back to their prospective countries is a terrifying prospect for many undocumented immigrants. This does not have to be the case. There are more civil and proper routes to take to allow undocumented immigrants to remain in this country and to give them the opportunity to adjust their status so that they can remain in this country legally.

So, how do we keep terrorists out without keeping out good people too? Immigration and refugee vetting needs to put the focus on point-of-entry procedures and protocols as well as background checks. I think it also should involve a *sharing of information* between countries for immigration purposes. If someone from a foreign country wishing to enter the United States has a criminal record, then we should be able to access that information from the country of the person seeking entry into the United States. This could be accomplished by a sharing of information between the United States and each individual country, or a collective sharing of information of all countries for the purpose of conducting background checks.

Stopping terrorists from entering the country is one thing, but stopping terrorism is quite a different matter. Our government does an outstanding job of stopping terrorist plots and threats to our nation. However, unfortunately some are successful, especially the lone wolves. I think that short of this country turning into military states with police and the military patrolling our city streets, to thwart and deter the type of lone wolf attacks that we have seen, we need to be vigilant and alert and remember to "say something" and to report anything or anyone who does not seem right or something that seems out of place.

Before, I talked about deterrence and having military as well as police patrolling our streets. Unfortunately, our world is changing, it *has* changed. Perhaps the time has come for police and military to occupy our city streets and keep the peace. Just the other day I watched the news about a terrorist attack and that evening, cable news reported that the stock markets were unaffected by the tragic events that occurred earlier in the day. One of the commentators even suggested that perhaps we are getting *accustomed* to terrorism occurring in our country. Are such events happening so frequently now that we as a nation are becoming desensitized to such tragic events? Is this now a sign of the times? Perhaps the face of America is changing, but we as a nation must grow stronger as a result of these changes. We and our country must never lose its identity and allow anyone or anything to destroy the foundation that our nation stands upon, or rip away the fabric that holds this great nation together.

CHAPTER 11

LGBT Awareness and Rights in America

The LGBT community has been fighting for the right to live and to enjoy the same rights as heterosexual couples. Same-sex couples should have the right to marry in every state, to adopt, to live and to work and utilize and patronize businesses and services without fear or apprehension of being discriminated against. Legislation needs to be uniform across states and each city and state needs to enforce the laws created on the government level.

We as Americans and we as human beings should have the right to live our lives in the way and in the manner that we choose within the confines of the law. Sexual preference and gender identification choice should not be dictated to anyone. Nonetheless, the LGBT community and those who are involved in same-sex relationships who choose to get married still have an uphill battle, as do those who are transgendered.

I think that part of the problem is a general lack of awareness and understanding of the transgendered community on the part of the public. A transgender person is defined as someone who lives as a member of a gender other than that which was assigned at birth and based on the anatomical sex of the person. It is also important to mention that a transgendered or *trans* person can be gay, bi-sexual, straight, queer any other sexual orientation. *Trans* individuals want to feel validated and accepted in society in each and every situation: at work, by family and friends and in society in general. Perhaps when society and each state finally recognizes and accepts transgendered individuals, then the trans community can feel validated once the rights and privileges of trans people and the LGBT community have been declared legal and officially acceptable.

At present, because that acceptance or lack of varies from state to state, it is difficult for a trans person or someone seeking same-sex marriage for instance to know if the laws are in favor of them or against them. Also, if a same-sex couple who marries in one state wants to move to a state that does not accept the idea of same-sex marriages, then they must re-consider their decision based in the lack of acceptance and uniformity in the laws of each state.

One such law or statute that has been a subject of controversy is the "Bathroom Bill" which defines access to public bathroom facilities such as restrooms by transgendered individuals. Critics of the bill state that access to public restrooms should only be dictated by the sex that is documented on an individual's birth certificate. The problem is that in addition to those trans people who are cross dressers, there are also people in transition and transsexuals who have already transitioned from being male to female through sex re-assignment surgery and hormone replacement therapy.

Essentially, this is new and uncharted territory. However, to continue to gain greater acceptance and promote awareness on a wider scale, the LGBT community needs to continue to make their voices heard and write to their senators and others to push for new legislation. The silence needs to be broken, envelopes need to be pushed to the limit and beyond and the concerns of the LGBT community must and will be heard until finally there is *universal* acceptance throughout the entire nation!

About the Author

David James Zoppi is an author and has written many books of varied genres.

David is also an award winning musician and has received the Liberace Keyboard

Entertainer Search award for the New England region, and the Louis Armstrong

Jazz award. David dedicates this book to his son Christopher David Zoppi.